A Breath of
Fresh Air

A Breath of
Fresh Air

Renie Smith

RESOURCE *Publications* · Eugene, Oregon

A BREATH OF FRESH AIR

Resource Publications
An Imprint of Wipf and Stock Publishers
199 W. 8th Ave., Suite 3
Eugene, OR 97401

www.wipfandstock.com

PAPERBACK ISBN: 978-1-7252-8571-2
HARDCOVER ISBN: 978-1-7252-8570-5
EBOOK ISBN: 978-1-7252-8572-9

Manufactured in the U.S.A.   11/18/20

This little book is dedicated to all my friends and family who have urged me for many years to publish some of my poems.

Contents

1. In General | 1

2. Celebrations | 21

3. Sorrow and Comfort | 31

4. Blessings | 51

5. Special Occasions | 61

6. Encouragement | 71

7. Just Me | 91

I AM A MOTHER, widow, grandmother and great grandmother. I began writing poems when I was a teenager but didn't do a lot with it until my children were grown. Since then I've written nearly 500, nearly all inspirational in nature, meant to encourage, comfort or entertain. I hope these will bless all who read them.

1

In General

At Calvary, I Was There

I was not there in person
When they nailed Him to the tree,
But my sin was placed upon Him
As He died for you and me.

I did not swing the hammer
That drove nails into His Hand,
I did not see His blood flow,
Or the darkness in the land.

But as He hung there on the cross
He looked down and saw me there,
Compassion shown in His eyes
As He said, "My child, I care."

He said, "I'm doing this for you,
To save you for all time.
My blood I shed, this pain I bear,
For you, my child, are mine."

So although it seems impossible,
In some ways I was there.
For me He suffered, bled and died,
To prove how much He cares.

Nails attached Him to the cross,
But they did not hold Him there.
T'was the love He had for you and me,
So we could be saved and His glory share.

Do I Trust Him?

I say I trust Him with my life,
That He'll protect me and provide,
I say He knows just what is best
And that He'll lead and guide.

So when dark clouds arise
And storms assault my days,
Do I trust Him and abide
Or do I question all His ways?

Does my soul cry out in fear
Or do I go to Him in prayer?
Do feel I'm all alone
Or remember that He is there?

If it doesn't face hard times,
My faith will never grow.
So I must learn to trust;
He'll see me through, I know.

I will grow much stronger still;
I'll learn to trust Him more.
He'll guide me and He'll lead me on
To that distant, golden shore.

Hard Times

You said there'd be hard times, Lord.
You said you'd see me through,
You said not to look at my circumstances,
To just remember to trust you.

I've read it in your Holy Word,
I know your Word is true,
But when things are all messed up,
I worry and forget to look to You.

Will I ever really learn, Lord?
Will I always panic and fret?
After all the times you've come through,
I seem to have not learned yet.

I'm sorry, Lord, that I keep forgetting,
That I look around me and stew,
I'll try really hard to remember
To trust you to really see me through.

His Purpose

God has a purpose for each life,
Every day and every hour,
He has things for us to do
and He supplies the Power.

Some tasks are simple and small,
Which we can quite easily do,
Others are much more difficult
and only His strength can see us through.

Some of the things we've done for Him
We really don't even know,
For He can use a simple kindness
His love and power to show.

He can use our obedience
To bless someone on our way,
We may never know who we've helped
As they struggled day after day.

So we need to be faithful
in all He bids us do,
and help as He directs us
and keep our hearts ever true

If Jesus Says

If Jesus says, (and He does),
That He'll be with us every day,
If Jesus says, (and He does,)
That He will guide us all the way.

If Jesus says, (and He does),
That He'll forgive our every sin,
If Jesus says, (and He does,)
He'll give us total peace within,

If Jesus says, (and He does),
That He loves us more than we could know,
If Jesus says, (and He does,)
He's washed and made us white as snow,

Then why do we, (and we do),
Constantly doubt and worry and fret?
Why do we, (and we do,)
Carry our burdens about like a pet?

Why do we, (and we do),
Grieve the heart of our dear Lord?
Why do we, (and we do,)
Fail to believe and trust in His Word?

If Jesus says, (and He does,)
Why isn't that enough for us?

My Heart's Desire

To know Him better and Love Him more
Is my heart's great desire,
To serve Him with a loving spirit
Whatever may transpire.

To know Him as well as He knows me
Won't happen here on earth,
But I'm promised that I'll be with Him
Because of my new birth.

But while I'm living here below
I need to serve Him well.
I need to walk and talk His love
So other folks can tell.

He knows I can't ever be perfect
And He gives me His help each day,
He guides me through each trial
And keeps my feet walking in His way.

My Only Hope

When where I am is scary,
When every road seems blocked,
When everywhere I turn
Every door is locked,

When the sun cannot pierce the clouds,
When all my world is black,
When my sleep has no peace or joy,
And I think God has turned His back.

Then the only way to look is up,
My only hope is Him,
For He it is who loves me so
And washed away my sin.

He is the one who knows my need
And knows what's best for me.
He is the one with power and grace
to truly set me free.

So when the sky is dark I know
to look to God above,
and trust Him to work all things out
and surround me with His love.

My Prayer

Oh, my Father, hear my prayer,
Keep me ever in Thy care,
Meet my needs this day, I pray,
And never, ever go away.

Teach me how to pray and live,
All myself to You I give,
Help me to never go astray,
But walk with You day after day.

Fill my heart with love for You,
Help me daily to be true,
Make me a blessing to others, Lord,
Help me to faithfully read your Word.

Keep me ever at your side,
Teach me to in You abide.
Take me home with you some day,
This is what I ask and pray.

Our Daily Goal

Knowing Him better and Loving Him more
Should be our goal every day.
Then He can teach and guide us
As we travel on our way.

He is not an angry, demanding God
We fearfully seek to appease.
He is a joyful, loving Dad
Who we cheerfully want to please.

He holds our future in His hands
As He faithfully meets our needs,
He is happy to take care of us,
We need not beg or plead.

Knowing that He loves us so
And tenderly holds us near,
Allows us to simply trust Him
And live daily with no dread or fear.

Our Father's Love

My daddy didn't love me more
The days that I was good,
But he was pleased when I behaved
The way he knew I should.

On days I needed a spanking,
He didn't love me less,
Be he had to help me
To become my very best.

It was my daddy's job
To help me grow up strong.
To be the person I should be,
I had to know right from wrong.

So it is for us with our
Heavenly Father above,
We don't always give Him pleasure,
But He always gives us love.

We may not walk obediently
and may grieve His heart today,
He will not give up on us,
Though we fail He will not turn away.

He is our Father and His love for us
Depends not on what we do,
But on who He is and what He did
On the cross for me and you.

Precious Thought

Precious thought—He loves me
and washed my sin away,
Always He is with me
Every night and day.

I don't deserve His love
But He loves me anyway,
He's come to dwell with me
and He says He's here to stay.

When I feel blue and lonely
He reminds me He is here,
Knowing He is with me always
Drives away all my fear.

Well He knows my sadness and pain
and the many tears I've cried,
Gently He reminds me
That for me He bled and died.

So daily I will trust Him
and bask in His marvelous love,
He will keep me always
Till He takes me home above.

The Gift of Love

Nothing I could ever do
Could get my sins forgiven.
Nothing I could ever do
Could get me into Heaven.

The best that I could offer
Wouldn't wash away my sin,
The best that I could offer
Wouldn't make me clean within.

All that I can ever do
Is accept this gift from You.
All that I can ever do
Is love You and be true.

Thank you for the gift You sent
From Heaven up above.
Thank you for the gift You sent,
The greatest gift of love.

The Long Goodbye

It's hard to lose our loved ones,
We miss them oh so much,
We miss their gentle hands
and their warm, loving touch.

But now they're still among us
Just don't know who we are,
Don't know our friends and neighbors
Who live both near and far,

They no longer share the memories
We've built through the years,
They look without seeing us
and we're reduced to tears.

It leaves us sad and lonely,
Not knowing what to do,
The house is just so empty,
our normal life is through.

They're leaving us behind,
a little more each day
And there is just no way
for them to choose to stay.

Tomorrow's Promise?

What tomorrow holds for me
I do not and can not know;
But I know my Savior is with me
and I know that He loves me so.

Whatever valley I walk through,
Whatever mountain I climb,
He never ever will leave me,
For I am His and He is mine.

This is not something I hope for,
It's what I know to be true.
The good news isn't for me alone,
It could be yours for He loves you, too.

Too Tired? Too Busy?

"I'm too tired to go to church,"
We're often heard to say.
But another invitation
Sees us merrily on our way.

"I'm to busy to read God's Word,
I don't have time to pray".
But a call from a friend,
And we chat the day away.

Just think how helpless and lost
We, all of us, would be,
If Jesus had been too busy and tired,
To die on the Cross for you and me.

Use Me, Lord

Help me to be kind, Lord,
To those I meet each day.
To share Your love and mercy
As they go along their way.

Use me, Lord, to bless them,
To brighten up their day,
So they will want to walk with You,
Your will and word obey.

Let me be a light, Lord,
A beacon to Your side,
So others will come to know you,
And in your love abide.

At the Door

He stood knocking at the door
His toolbox at his feet,
Many repairs were needed inside
But the owner he had yet to meet.

No one came and opened the door,
No one invited him in,
He wasn't allowed to make repairs,
Or save this person from sin.

It wasn't His way to force the door,
Or enter the house uninvited,
If only they would ask Him in,
He'd enter and be so delighted.

So many repairs were needed,
All the hurts and cries from the past.
If only they'd ask Him He would give
A peace and a joy that would last.

Is this your heart's door where He waits,
With your grief and your tears inside?
Open the door wide and ask Him in,
It was for your sins He died.

2

Celebrations

Christmas Time

It's Christmas time again,
A time for peace and joy,
A time to remember Mary
And her precious baby boy.

A time to think of why He came,
To save us all from sin,
A time to open up our hearts
And let the Savior in.

As you think of family
And friends both near and far,
Come to Him like the wise men did
Who followed that bright star.

Let Him be your Savior
Your healer, your friend
His love is true and He'll be
With you through the end.

Christmas and Easter

Christmas and Easter
are the same story,
How Jesus came down
to us from glory.

How He left His home
in Heaven above,
Was born as a baby
to show us His love.

Then one day He died
for us on the cross,
That we might be saved
and our souls not be lost.

Then He arose.
Over death He had won!
Our wonderful Savior!
God's obedient Son.

The New Marriage

"It is not good," our Maker said,
"For man to dwell alone."
He knew we all need someone
To share our life and make a home.

For life is never easy,
And people can be cruel.
Often those we think are friends,
Can make us look the fool.

We need to shut the cold world out,
To be safe and warm inside;
We need to find our soul mate,
Man needs to find his bride.

God saw Floyd, alone and lost,
And knew his heart was breaking,
He had no one to talk to
And his empty arms were aching.

So God blessed Floyd, and Dolores, too,
And gave them to each other.
We pray his blessings on you both,
Our sister and our brother.

The Plan

Satan thought he knew a way
To spoil God's wondrous plan,
Destroy the perfect Lamb of God,
who was sent down to save man.

When Jesus died on the cross
Satan was filled with glee-
He thought he'd won and man
Was doomed to hell for all eternity.

Imagine his surprise and dismay
when Jesus arose from the grave.
All his hopes were dashed and gone
and Heaven gave God all the praise.

So as we rejoice in the resurrection
On this most blessed Easter day,
We also rejoice that the Devil's plan
Is thwarted every time we pray.

Can You Know?

Do you think you can learn, if you try,
Just where you will go, when you die?

Do you think that it all will depend
On exactly how good you have been?

Do you think you must wait to see
What God's judgment on your life will be?

What if you knew you could know
Right now, where you'll be when you go?

If you didn't have to wait 'til you die
To know you'd be with Jesus on high?

If you could go to your bed every night
Knowing you and your God were 'all right'?

Well, that's the gift of Easter day,
You can know your sins are washed away.

You can be sure, it's in His Word,
That He's your Savior, Master, Lord.

A Wedding Blessing

May this day mark the beginning
Of a beautiful new life together,
May you have joyous sunny days
Along with the cloudy weather.

May your love grow strong through the years,
As you share both the joy and the tears.
May your lives be truly blest,
May you look to the Lord for your rest.

May you always be lovers and friends,
Loyal to the very end.
May God bless the vows that you make,
And guide every step that you take.

Baby Dedication

You bring your son unto the Lord
As did Hannah of old,
And pray that God will bless
And help his character to mold.

May he be a blessing to you,
This beautiful little boy,
And may he grow into a child
Who'll fill your hearts with joy.

May you find the strength you need
To be firm, yet loving and kind.
That he will learn to do his best
With both his body and mind.

So on this day we ask that God
Send blessings from above,
To be with you each-wherever you are,
And to keep you in His love.

Brenda, the Graduate

You worked hard and studied long,
And burned the midnight oil.
No one did this for you,
For this you had to toil.

You did it through the surgeries,
Through sick kids in the night.
Through subjects that were difficult,
But it turned out all right.

We're proud of all that you've achieved,
That you didn't ever quit.
You stuck with it, though it was hard,
Now, You're a graduate!!!

3

Sorrow and Comfort

A Day to Remember

This is the day he left you
Alone and sad and blue.
You'll be together again someday,
Or course, you know that's true.

But in this life down here below,
You miss him oh so much.
You'd love to have him here with you,
To feel his loving touch.

The memories help a little
But often they bring tears
As you recall the times you shared
Through all those many years.

God knows the heartache you still feel,
And He will not leave your side,
He's with you every day and night
As you in Him abide.

So share your tears with Jesus
And tell Him all your cares
And know that others hold you up
Before the Throne in prayer.

God of Comfort

May God, the God of all Comfort,
Hold you close to His loving breast,
May you feel His arms around you,
Filling you with peace and rest.

May you know that He is faithful,
That His love for you is true,
That He never would forsake you,
But He's always there with you.

In these days and nights of sorrow,
When your heart is full of grief,
Let His loving grace surround you
And give you peace and sweet relief.

Going Forward in His Love

He loves you so, I'm sure you know,
But I want to remind you.
Wherever you go, Whatever you do,
That He's right there beside you.

He's faithful always to the end,
In good times and in bad,
It's easy to see that when we're happy,
Much harder to see when we're sad.

His love for you will never fail,
He says He'll never leave you;
You may not feel it but it's true,
Don't let the devil deceive you.

As you go forward with your life,
And try to do your best,
Get your strength and direction from Him,
And let Him take care of the rest.

He loves you so, you're precious to Him,
He knows your thoughts and fears,
Trust Him daily and you'll see
His faithfulness through the years.

Gone from Us, Present with Christ

Released from her prison of pain and fear,
Her soul flew home to Jesus' open arms.
Free of the body that crumbled and hurt,
She is safely away from all sorrow and harms.

She will be greatly missed, of course,
As a wife and companion, a mother, a friend,
Grandchildren will not remember her love,
The void she leaves will never end.

But we would not wish her back
To a tortured life controlled by pain.
Our hearts ache that she's gone,
But our loss is definitely her gain.

The Nature of Grief

Sometimes grief brings people together,
Sometimes it drives them apart,
It's because they cannot understand
What is in the other one's heart.

Sometimes the sorrow combined
Seems too much for either to bear,
But sometimes it's a great comfort
To have someone with whom to share.

If you can't share your grief with a loved one,
Then share it with someone who'll care,
Who can listen to your heart breaking,
And assure you He'll always be there.

A grief not shared can drive you insane,
It can tear your whole world apart.
Don't keep it inside, to eat you up,
Let Jesus comfort and heal your heart.

His Passing

He crossed the line from here to there,
Walked into his Lord's loving arms.
He left all behind of his life here,
He is safe from all ill and harms.

God called, he answered; What else could he do?
With Him is where he's meant to be.
He's created to worship and love his dear Lord,
And forever His glory he'll see.

You'll see him again when you join him there,
He'll know you like he knew you here.
You'll join in and worship together
The Savior we all hold so dear.

So think of him, remember and miss him,
Acknowledge the great loss you feel.
Don't sorrow as if it's all over,
For eternity with him will be real.

Think fondly of times had together,
Smile and laugh at funny things past.
Always remember, the love you all shared,
Isn't over; it always will last.

In the Loss of a Spouse

He said we would become one flesh
Our will no longer our own.
So, surely when one half is gone,
He knows we feel alone.

He fashioned us to love this way,
With all our heart and soul.
He knew with this togetherness
We'd be but parts of one whole.

Though the separation will be short
It seems much longer to us here.
He'll never leave us on our own,
But will lead us away from all fear.

So though our steps may falter
We should look to Him in prayer.
For He will never leave or fail us
He'll surround us with His loving care.

Losing a Child

Losing a child seems so unnatural,
It's not the way it should be,
If we could bargain with our God
We'd cry, "Not him, Lord, take me."

I know your hearts are saddened
And you'd like to understand,
But God doesn't usually explain,
Just says, 'trust and take my hand.'

Lean on His shoulder and cry your tears,
He knows the sorrow you feel,
He'll be your comfort and your hope,
Your broken hearts He'll heal.

Losing a Grandchild

I cannot imagine the horror
Of losing a grandchild you love,
Even knowing you'll see him again
And be reunited with God up above.

The memories of him as a baby,
As a toddler learning to walk,
The cute things he said that made
You laugh as he began to talk.

His excitement when he learned to read
And shared with you each new book.
When he came home from school with his
Report card . . . and let you look.

All the times he called to tell you
What he just couldn't wait to share,
The hugs that always let you know
He was so glad that you were there.

May these memories bring you comfort
In the coming months and days,
As you thank God for the time you had,
As you go to Him with praise.

He understands the hurt you feel,
He knows your hearts are sad.
But if you'll let Him hold you close,
He'll comfort and make you glad.

You'll always miss your boy
And wish he was still here.
You'll go on loving him each day
And remembering him, so dear.

But let your Father heal your hearts
And take the pain away.
Be comforted in knowing
You'll see him again some day.

Losing a Parent

Losing a parent is a hard thing to bear,
It leaves us feeling alone.
But God will comfort and guide us,
For He lovingly cares for His own.

Our minds are filled with memories
Of days and years gone by.
We remember the good and the bad times
And tears of remorse fill our eyes.

Cherish the good times, let the bad memories fade,
Know their love for you was true.
Take God's comfort and peace to your heart
Let Him show how much He loves you.

Missing Her

She's dancing with Jesus on streets of gold,
In a body that's well and will never grow old.
She's in the presence of her Savior and Lord,
Experiencing the joys described in His Word.

She'll welcome us all when we go home,
To a place so grand we'll nevermore roam.
But we'll miss her greatly here below,
Until, soon, to Heaven we too will go.

God Understands

God understands your sorrow,
He knows your heavy heart.
He's there to give you comfort
And He never will depart.

May His presence comfort you
And may His love enfold you.
Now and ever after
May His strong arms hold you.

Our Dad

Why, God, did you take our dad away?
Why didn't you heal him and let him stay?

We're just kids and we need our dad,
He was the best father we could have had.

We'll miss our dad, Oh God, You know,
Why couldn't he stay and watch us grow?

He won't be here to teach us to drive,
Why didn't You heal him and keep him alive?

He won't see us graduate from school,
I'm sorry, God, but that just seems cruel.

We're trying to trust but we don't understand;
You could have touched him with Your mighty hand.

Please help us remember that Your love is real,
and You'll never leave us no matter how we feel.

Take care of us, God, it's up to You now
To get us through this though we don't see how.

Sorrow for your loss

When sorrow and grief invade our life,
We wish for days without sadness and strife.
When death takes a loved one from our side,
We long for a safe place to run and hide.
When grief overwhelms us and bows us low,
We yearn for a haven where we could go.
When at last we relent and ask God in,
He'll comfort us and save us from sin.
So give Him your burdens, tears, and grief,
He'll fill you with peace and give sweet relief.

He did not cause this grief,
Nor did He bring this loss.
He loves you for eternity,
He proved that with the cross.

Still Missing Him

When you promised to love him forever,
To be true until death would you part,
You had no way of knowing how long
After death he would still hold your heart.

Though he is gone you will never forget him,
His dreams will live on in your own.
Your kids and grandkids will remember
His love long after they're grown.

The years that you two spent together
Learning and loving each day,
Will sustain you throughout your tomorrows
As you travel this uncertain way.

May the memories that you built together
Bring you comfort in the dark night.
May the dreams that you shared give you courage
To go forward and walk toward the light.

Thanksgiving into Christmas

Thanksgiving was a lonely time
And Christmas now draws near.
I miss you so, my darling,
How I wish that you were here.

I remember Christmases we shared
And good times through the years.
I can't see the tree or lights clearly
As my eyes fill up with tears.

I know that you are happy there
And your suffering and pain are gone.
Some day my heart will beat again
And my spirit will sing and be strong.

But now, my dear, I feel so lost
I miss you each night and day.
My world will never be the same
Since that night you went away.

Lonely Anniversary

Thirty years ago you wed
and promised to be true.
The love you shared still lingers,
Though he's not there with you.

You gave him everything you had,
You were a loving wife.
Together you raised your family
and built a happy life.

Then he got sick and life became
a roller coaster ride,
He endured treatments and pain
But you were by his side.

Now you celebrate this day alone
Without the man you love,
Remember, he's not really gone,
He's waiting up above.

4

Blessings

A Gift from God

A new little baby in your life,
A wee one to hold and to love,
A wondrous and precious gift
Sent down from Heaven above.

Your life will never be the same,
He'll require your attention and care,
You never, ever want to fail him,
But always, for him, to be there.

He'll wrap you around his finger,
Keep your heart in his little hand,
You'll love him so much it hurts,
And obey his every command.

So, hang on for the ride of your life,
Tumbling down 'Grandparent Way',
You'll laugh, cry, but never be bored,
And you'll love him more every day.

A Heart of Gratitude

Give me a heart of gratitude, Lord,
Help me not to grumble or fuss,
Make me truly thankful
For all the ways you bless us.

Help me to see how much we have,
And how much others need,
Let me share and help provide
Food and water and seed.

I don't deserve these blessings, Lord,
No more than others do.
Help me, Father, to share your love
In everything I say and do.

Grandma and Grandpa

So now you're Grandma, and Grandpa, too
My heartfelt congrats to both of you.
New little ones to hold and love,
Gifts from our Father in Heaven above.

Little ones who'll love you and give you hugs,
And show you the flowers and little bugs,
Children who'll show you life through their view
Who'll always be fun with arms out to you.

So enjoy them, love them & spoil them some, too,
That's why God gave them to you!

New Baby

I'm sure this little baby
Has turned your lives around
You could not have imagined
The happiness you've found

You could never have guessed
You would love him so much
That your heart would leap
At his smile, his touch.

He's got you, you know,
You're hooked for life.
You're a family now
Not just husband & wife.

So, hang on for the ride
Some days may be long
But you'll get through it all,
With love you can't go wrong.

The Best Baby

Our grandchild is born,
We're happy, we're glad.
It's the easiest baby
We've ever had.

No morning sickness,
At least not for us.
No backache, no classes,
No problems, no fuss.

No getting up nights
With babies to feed,
No dirty diapers,
We like this, indeed!

This is so much easier
Than when ours were small.
Maybe it's because, now,
We really do know it all!

Welcome, Baby

A new little life at your house,
A new child to nurture and love.
A sweet little baby so perfect,
You know she's a gift from above.

She'll grow into a young lady
Far faster than you could know.
But she'll always be very special,
So enjoy her and watch her grow.

A Wedding Blessing

May this day mark the beginning
Of a beautiful new life together,
May you have joyous sunny days
Along with the cloudy weather.

May your love grow strong through the years,
As you share both the joy and the tears.
May your lives be truly blest,
May you look to the Lord for your rest.

May you always be lovers and friends,
Loyal to the very end.
May God bless the vows that you make,
And guide every step that you take.

Bless This Marriage

Father, not just he and she
But he and she and Thee;
For a marriage to succeed
This is how it must be.

As these here make their vows
And promise to be true,
Help them to remember
To give first place to You.

For only as you lead them
And teach them to obey,
Can they build a marriage
That grows stronger every day.

Bless them, Father, on this day
And each day that's to come,
So they can build a family
And make their house a home.

5

Special Occasions

Happy 75th Birthday

75 years is a long time to live,
To learn how to love and to share and to give,
A time to experience what God's love can do,
To learn to appreciate how much He loves you.
To be a good neighbor, a grandpa, a friend,
To prepare for the next life which never will end.

But it's a short time, too,
To try to do all you wanted to.
A short time to learn all you wanted to know,
Not long enough to go where you wanted to go.
We have only the days He chooses to give,
So we must stay busy with learning to live.

Forty Nine!

So you're forty nine! Big deal!
I suppose you think that's old,
It's kind of relative, I think,
Kind of like hot and cold.

To some folks you're still quite young
But your kids probably disagree,
They think you're ancient history,
But you're still young to me.

So don't despair, enjoy your day,
Have some cake and ice cream.
Each year passes more quickly,
At least that's how it will seem.

Enjoy the time you have here now,
With your family and friends,
This stage of life won't last,
All too soon it ends.

Soon your kids will move on
And you won't see them much,
You'll be kept quite busy
Electronically keeping in touch.

So even though those times are hard
And you long for earlier days,
Remember God loves you and yours
And He'll guide you in His ways.

Happy Birthday

Ninety-five years of life on this earth,
So many years since the day of your birth,
Times of joy, gladness, sorrow and pain,
That you wouldn't want to live over again.

Years of learning that God is faithful,
That His love and grace are ever true,
And that He holds you near and dear.
Til you go home, He'll see you through.

Fifty Years Together

Fifty years ago this day,
you promised to be true
Before your friends and family
You both said, 'I Do."

You said you'd stick together
Through good times and through bad
You'd share the laughter and the tears
The happy and the sad.

You'd be each others' best support
Their private cheering squad.
And make your marriage as it was
Designed to be, by God.

Now kids are grown and on their own,
The house shelters just you two,
But the love you share together
Still burns bright and true.

Turning 65

You've reached the age of sixty five,
That's quite a few years to be alive,
Years to live, to learn, to grow,
To develop seeds you now can sow.

But years ahead to serve your Lord,
To lean more heavily on his Word,
To be an elder, a mentor, a friend,
To serve wherever He shall send.

When all your earthly work is done,
The battles over and victories won,
When you bow before the throne of Grace,
And gaze on His beloved face,

Then the years you lived here below,
Won't matter, they'll fade to 'long ago.'
But you're still here, so be alive!
And celebrate that you're sixty five!

To the Bride and Groom

You come to be joined as man and wife,
You promise to nurture each other for life.
It will not be easy for life is a trial,
The easiest part is the walk down the aisle.

But Jesus is with you, you're not on your own,
His Word says He never will leave us alone.
Make Him your partner, house guest and guide,
Your marriage will flourish with Him by your side.

Happy Mother's Day to Us

Mothers we are and always will be
Beyond our days on this earth.
For we became mothers, you see
The very first time we gave birth.

We love our kids, pray for them,
And teach them to be their best.
That's all we can do. We trust
God to take care of the rest.

Then grand babies come,
So very sweet to hold,
They grow up pretty fast
And we know we're growing old.

Then the greats' come along
Which really blows our mind.
As we count all our blessings
We see that God is so very kind.

6

Encouragement

Trash to Treasure

From our trash He can make treasure,
He can heal each hurt and woe.
He can turn our clouds to sunshine,
If only to Jesus we will go.

He's aware each time we falter,
He knows we can't make the mark.
But He can use the sad time, bad time,
Even when our way seems dark.

What we scorn our Lord may cherish,
What we hate He has plans to use;
All the trash we so despair of,
Can be made precious by our Lord.

He knows every trial before us,
Knows each burden we will bear,
He will help us, lead us, guide us
If we go to Him in Prayer.

Too Bad to Be Forgiven?

Remember the thief on the Cross,
He hung there by Jesus side,
Jesus forgave all of his sin,
Though he'd stolen and probably lied.

There is no limit, no degree of sin
That God cannot or will not forgive,
Jesus died to cleanse us all,
And take us to Heaven to live.

Are 'small' sins are as bad as big ones?
In God's sight they're all the same.
The only thing He cannot forgive
Is if we reject and refuse His dear name.

So come to Him now for He loves you,
He wants to save you from sin.
He wants you to end up in Heaven
To spend all of eternity with Him.

The Liar

The devil comes to each of us
and says, "You are not loved.
No one truly cares for you,
on earth or up above.

No one sees the hurt and pain
that dwells within your heart.
You're on your own in this big world,
No one will take your part."

But he's a liar, this we know—
He cannot speak what's true,
But God is truth and He has proved
How much He truly loves you.

Each of us is His dear child,
When He dwells within our heart.
He will not ever let us go,
From us He'll never part.

Spring Will Come

Beneath the cold hard ground
Under all the ice and snow
Are the bulbs and seeds we planted,
Flowers—just waiting to grow.

The trees now so barren and dead
Are just sleeping and waiting for spring,
For the cue from the sunshine and rain
To leaf out while the birds come to sing.

The world looks deserted and brown,
With no sign of cheer for our heart,
Spring is the real resurrection,
And we can't wait to see it all start.

Our lives, too, seem to have seasons,
Some full of sorrow and loss,
Others seem happy and joyous,
Like Spring with the love of the cross.

So when life all around us seems crazy,
When we can't see the flowers and grass,
We cling to God's grace and mercy,
Knowing that this season, too, will pass.

Slow Down & Catch Up

Are you running from God,
Instead of going His way?
Are you going in circles?
Do you dread each new day?

As the world rushes by
Do the noises you hear
Drown out the still voice
Of the One who's so dear?

Do you need to slow down,
To step back and be still,
And not venture forward
Til you know His sweet will?

Let Him order your steps
And guide you each day,
Let Him be your friend,
He's with you to stay.

When you spend time with Him,
When you worship and pray,
He'll restore your peace,
He'll show you the way.

Our Daily Grace

He gives Grace to us daily,
As we struggle on our way,
We know He'll never leave us,
But is with us day by day.

He helps us through the hard times,
And gives us good days, too.
We know we can depend on Him,
And that His word is true.

We know He'll never leave us,
But is always by our side,
He'll lead us ever upward,
To Heaven He'll be our guide.

He Is Here

If Jesus came in person
And stood right by your side,
Would you find it easier
To trust Him and abide?

If you could reach out
And hold His gentle hand
Would you simply praise Him
Or would you still demand?

If you could see His face
And feel His loving arms,
Would you know He cares,
And will protect you from all harms?

He is just as present
As if His voice we heard,
He will never leave us,
He says so in His Word.

His Promise

This He has promised
and this He will do,
He will be there
and take care of you.

Never to leave you,
nor ever depart,
He'll hold you close
Right in His Heart.

He won't walk away,
He'll never forsake,
He'll love you always
for His name's sake.

God is so awesome,
His love is so true,
He sent His son
to die for you.

He Already Knows

God never wrings His hands
and says, "what am I to do?"
He doesn't struggle to figure out
an answer for me and you.

He is not surprised at our troubles
though they may surely startle us,
He already knows the solution.
We are the ones who worry and fuss.

If we could only remember
Our loving Lord is on the throne
He'll care for our earthly needs
Until finally He'll call us home.

He Keeps Holding On

Jesus holds my hand,
He'll never let me fall.
His hold is sure, He won't let go
So on Him I daily call.

If I hold onto Him
I could stumble and let go
But in His hands I'm safe,
He'll hold me tight, I know.

Like a parent holds a child's hand
To help them on the way,
So I won't fall, He'll hold me close
And keep me day by day.

He Knows

God knows our hearts, and our hurts,
He knows exactly how we feel.
He stays close to us to prove
His love for us is real.

He doesn't always take the pain
But gives us strength to bear it,
He surrounds us with loving friends
So we can learn to share it.

Never does He leave our side,
Nor are our tears a waste,
Always He is with us
When we run to Him in haste.

We can't really understand
Why He permits such sorrows,
We can only trust Him and know
He holds all of our tomorrows.

He's Waiting

Outside your heart's door He stands
Knocking to be invited in,
There is no knob that He can turn,
So He waits to redeem you from sin.

He's done all that He can do,
He died to set you free,
His love sent Him to the cross,
He wants to save both you and me.

The ball is in your court, now,
You decide what you will do,
Whether to let Him come inside:
The choice is up to you.

Goodbye and God Bless You

God has a plan for everyone
To take us through this life.
His plan includes our family;
Our children and husband or wife.

Sometimes His plan keeps us near
The ones we love the best,
Sometimes He takes us far away,
From the east to the west.

Wherever He has us live and work,
One thing is always true;
He is with us for He said,
"I will never leave you."

So as you leave us and move on
To the next stage of His plan,
Our love and prayers go with you,
And we'll meet again in the promised land.

Good Enough for Heaven?

No, you're not good enough,
And I could never be;
That's why Jesus Christ came,
To make a way for you and me.

We can try with all our might
To be good enough to get in
But Jesus is the only way
To be forgiven of all our sin.

Our Holy God said that no sin,
No matter how tiny or small,
Could enter in His Heaven;
There could be no sin at all.

So Jesus came and gave his life
And died that we may live.
Will we accept the greatest gift
That God could ever give?

When you stand before the judgment seat
And hear your guilt proclaimed,
It will be too late to cry and plead,
Too late to clear your name.

God Has A Plan for Us

God has a plan for everyone,
He knows our every breath;
He knows what we'll accomplish
and when our eyes will close in death.

He knows the friends we'll have in life,
He knows who and if we'll marry.
He knows the talents that we have
And every burden we will carry.

Some of us will live many years
To finish the work He wants done.
Some will complete their tasks early in life
And go home, their victory won.

None of us knows, in sickness or health
When our time on earth is done.
We must live each day in obedience
And wait for Him to call us home.

God Is with You

God is with you every day,
Leading you along the way,
He will never leave your side,
If you still in Him abide.

Though your path is hard right now
Before His throne you humbly bow,
Cast all your care on Him above,
Let Him show you His great love.

Let him lead you in His way,
Guide each step you take today,
Remember He is always near,
He knows all your hurt and fear.

When your heart is scared and cold
Come to Him, Be brave! Be bold!
God will always answer prayer,
He will never cease to care.

Dark dark days and long long nights
Fill our hearts with dread and fright,
He knows our cares, our fears, our heart,
He will never, ever depart.

A Blessed Life

I'm blessed though my way is hard,
No easy road for me.
Although my life is difficult,
I know from sin I am set free.

I learn the lessons from my Lord,
Though my learning is quite slow.
But I know my Lord is with me,
Wherever I may go.

Although my body needs His touch,
My spirit needs it more.
It's far more important that I arrive
On that Heavenly shore.

I'd rather suffer here below
Than have Him heal me now,
If healing me might make me miss
The path He has laid out.

So, though my life's not easy
And I suffer much with pain,
I'll bear it here as He gives grace
And concentrate on Heavenly gain

7

Just Me

Beauty Is in the Eye

They were finally ready to bloom,
I'd raised them all from seeds,
But my son-in-law pulled them,
He thought they were weeds!

Expired

My driver's License! Oh No!
I'd forgotten to check the date.
I ran right down to renew it
They were closed—I was too late.

Then I thought—it's just as well
With my hair straight I looked a fright.
I'd wash and curl it tonight
So tomorrow it would look just right.

I checked my makeup and combed my hair,
I knew I looked my very best.
But they didn't take my picture
'cause I flunked the stupid test!

It's Relative

I'm okay about growing older,
'Grandma' suits me just fine,
It's that I'm a 'mother-in-law'
That really blows my mind.

My Flowers

I gaze upon my flower bed,
Covered deeply with snow,
And I begin to wonder
Where did my flowers go?

I know such things of beauty
Are not now simply dead,
Beneath the ground they prepare
To bloom in the Spring ahead.

In spring they'll poke their heads
Up from the ground below,
And make my world a nicer place,
Until it starts to snow.

Send 'em Home

Congressmen and senators
Are sent to do our will,
To carry our concerns and needs
as they meet on Capital Hill.

We send them there
To do what we want done,
They don't seem to understand,
They only know they won.

Now they get to move to DC,
and live life in a faster pace,
They do what they want and forget us
Until their next political race.

We need to send them home again,
To live with the laws they wrote,
And send someone new to Washington
Who'll remember how they got our vote.

The Fat Man Cometh

The fat man is coming soon
with reindeer on the fly.
He never stops at my house
and I would like to know why.

It can't be that I misbehave,
I'm much too old for that.
Perhaps the cookies aren't enough
or maybe he hates my cat.

Every year he skips our house,
Flies merrily past our place.
I wish he'd stop so we could meet
and I could ask him face to face,

"Who do you think you are,
Skipping me every year.
Why even in Macy's parade,
You're relegated to the rear.

You're really not all that great,
No matter how special you feel.
Actually you're quite presumptuous,
Considering that you're not even real."

The New Kid

Mom said we're getting a new kid,
And it might be a girl or a boy,
I'm gonna have to share with him,
My room, my bed, and my favorite toy.

But when I asked more about him,
Mom said she didn't know.
That we'd have to wait to see
If it's a Becky or a Beau.

But I had many questions
And I kept getting bolder.
"So tell me mom, will this kid
Be about my age . . . or older?"

The Remote

I pushed the little button and waited to see
If the TV would come on,
It didn't, so I tried it again
And wondered what was wrong.

I pushed some other buttons,
But the television stayed black,
Why wouldn't this thing work,
What talent did I lack?

I waved the controller around
And shook it up a bit,
Then I saw I was pointing it
At me, instead of it.

Too, Too Much

Too old for a sitter
But too young to date,
Too old to trick or treat
Too young to come in late

Always too fat,
Never, ever too thin,
Stuck in the middle
With no way to win.

Now as I'm older
I know it's still so,
Whatever I'm doing
I'm always too slow.

Too young for discounts
Too old to be hired,
Not ready for Medicare,
But, boy am I tired.

My whole life has been
Quite simply, too much,
So just leave me alone,
I'm too fragile to touch.

The Empty Nest

Saying good-bye is always hard
It's never easy to let them go.
But they're all grown up now—
You've taught them what they need to know.

Oh, they'll still learn, as we all must
They'll make choices wrong and right,
To protect them, you'd really like
To draw them near and hold on tight.

But off they go and you shed tears,
It will never be the same again;
Visits will be great, always too short,
To keep in touch, you use your pen.

They won't write much, they'll call sometimes,
They'll be busy with friends you don't know,
But this is what you raised them to do
So, say good-bye, and off they go!

My Plans

Oh, I planned my day so carefully,
I dotted every 'i' and crossed every 't';
As my day passed I learned what mattered
Was what God wanted, not me.

Every 'mistake' served His purpose,
Each interruption was part of His plan,
What I had envisioned did not happen,
I had to let Him have command.

When I yielded myself to His leading,
Let Him order my day and my night,
I found I could do what He wanted,
In His strength and in His own might.

Mothers

Mothers are not perfect,
Not every mom is grand,
We do our best and hope
Someday our kids will understand.

It's hard, as a mom, to see
Your child make a bad choice.
Sometimes the hardest thing to do
Is to still that warning voice.

We love them and we guide them
the best way we know how,
We teach them about Jesus
And hope their knees will bow.

As they grow up and need us less
and turn from us to their friends,
It's easy to think our role as a mom
Is drawing to an early end.

But we'll always be their mothers,
When we've grown old and gray,
We'll never stop loving them,
And every day we'll pray.

And as we bounce their children
On our bony old knees,
We'll whisper to the Father
To keep them safe, please.

Memories

Remember back when you were a child
And things were so simple and true,
Dad went to work, the kids to school,
And Mom stayed home to take care of you.

The streets were safe, your house secure,
You could play out at night until dark.
Your favorite place to be after school
Was down the street at the baseball park.

Coke came in bottles and so did milk;
The mailman knew everyone's name.
At night after supper when homework was done,
The kids came outside to play one last game.

Now those days are gone, life sure has changed,
And I'm not so sure, for the better.
But the memories we have of when we were young
Will stay with us forever and ever.

Love Is . . .

To a baby, it's mother's breast
To the weary, a day of rest.

To mother it's a sticky kiss,
To the teen, a fair haired miss.

To grandma it's the phone ringing,
For Uncle Joe the birds are singing.

For the homeless, it's a clean bed
And a pillow to lay their head.

For the hungry it's food to eat,
For the lonely, a friend to meet.

For some it's a hand to hold
As they face the trials of growing old.

It can be a touch, a smile
That makes a day seem worthwhile.

For each it's what we most need,
From the smallest to the greatest deed.

Love is all these things and more,
It can't be purchased from a store.

It springs from deep within the soul,
Love is what makes each of us whole.

Make a Difference

Do a random act of kindness
As you go about your day,
Be a blessing unto others,
Spread some joy along the way.

Many folks are steeped in sadness
And have burdens hard to bear,
Many fear each new tomorrow
And have no one there to care.

Your smile may lift their spirits,
Your kind words may touch their heart.
If you but stop to offer help
They may make a brand new start.

You cannot know how much you help,
Your deeds might be unknown,
But God, who sees and knows it all,
Will smile on you from His throne.

Growing Older

Growing old is not for sissies,
To that I can truly attest;
What used to be 'poor effort'
May soon become my best.

My body seems to fall apart,
It's crumbling as I write.
And the way my eyes are going,
Things may soon be 'out of sight'.

As my body loses strength
and I slow down day by day,
I'm thankful that my mind's still here
And I fervently pray it will stay.

But when all is said and done
and my life here is no more,
I know my Lord will welcome me
On that distant beautiful shore.

Til then He'll keep me day by day,
and guide each step I take.
I will not have to walk alone,
For me He'll not forsake.

Friends

'Old friends are best', we often say
But we treasure the new as well,
New friends know what we've shown them,
Old friends know secrets they could tell.

New friends make our life richer,
They add spice to our every day,
Old friends are the core of our support,
And they never will go away.

New friends know our kids as they're grown,
They know all our grandkids, too.
Old friends remember our babies and tots,
They know what we've been through.

New friends are in our lives today
We value the love they give.
Old friends are in our hearts and our minds,
For as long as we both shall live.

So, Thank God for all our friends,
Old friends and new friends, too.
In case I haven't said it before,
You're my dear friend and I love you.

www.ingramcontent.com/pod-product-compliance
Lightning Source LLC
Chambersburg PA
CBHW070503090426
42735CB00012B/2664